Contents

KT-116-184

What is a leader? 4

Ways to be a good leader 6

Activity. 22

Picture glossary 23

Index 24

Being a leader means taking charge.

Citizenship

Being a Leader

Cassie Mayer

Heinemann
LIBRARY

www.heinemann.co.uk/library
Visit our website to find out more information about Heinemann Library books.

To order:
 Phone 44 (0) 1865 888066
 Send a fax to 44 (0) 1865 314091
Visit the Heinemann Bookshop at www.heinemann.co.uk/library to browse our catalogue and order online.

First published in Great Britain by Heinemann Library, Halley Court, Jordan Hill, Oxford OX2 8EJ, part of Harcourt Education. Heinemann is a registered trademark of Harcourt Education Ltd.

© Harcourt Education Ltd 2007
First published in paperback in 2008
The moral right of the proprietor has been asserted.

All rights reserved. No part of this publication may be reproduced, stored in a retrieval system, or transmitted in any form or by any means, electronic, mechanical, photocopying, recording, or otherwise, without either the prior written permission of the publishers or a licence permitting restricted copying in the United Kingdom issued by the Copyright Licensing Agency Ltd, 90 Tottenham Court Road, London W1T 4LP (www.cla.co.uk).

Editorial: Cassie Mayer and Charlotte Guillain
Design: Joanna Hinton-Malivoire
Illustrated by Mark Beech
Art editor: Ruth Blair
Production: Duncan Gilbert

Printed and bound in China by South China Printing Co. Ltd.

ISBN 978 0 431 18677 1 (hardback)
11 10 09 08 07
10 9 8 7 6 5 4 3 2 1

ISBN 978 0 431 18685 6 (paperback)
12 11 10 09 08
10 9 8 7 6 5 4 3 2 1

British Library Cataloguing in Publication Data
Mayer, Cassie
Being a leader. - (Citizenship)
1. Leadership - Juvenile literature
I. Title
158.4
A full catalogue record for this book is available from the British Library

Being a leader means setting
a good example.

When you help someone ...

you are being a good leader.

When you take charge ...

you are being a good leader.

When you invite other
children to join in ...

you are being a good leader.

When you ask other children how
they feel ...

you are being a good leader.

When you praise other people …

you are being a good leader.

When you keep trying and do
not give up …

you are being a good leader.

When you give other children
a turn to lead ...

you are being a good leader.

It is important to be a good leader.

How can you be a good leader?

Activity

How is this girl being a good leader?

Picture glossary

 **leader** someone who takes charge

 **praise** to tell someone you think they did a good job

Index

ask 12

help 6

invite 10

praise 14

take charge 4, 8

take turns 18

Note to Parents and Teachers

Before reading
Ask the children if they know what it means "to be a leader". Explain that a good leader is someone who helps other people. Ask them if they think they would like to be a leader.

After reading
• Play "Follow my leader". Tell the children to follow you in a line and to do exactly what you do. Then ask the children to nominate a new leader. Point out that a good leader lets others have a turn.
• Joining in game: Teach the children the Nursery rhyme *The farmer's in his den*. Tell the children to make a circle and to sing the rhyme. They should choose a farmer and then let the farmer choose a wife, child, dog and finally gently all pat the dog.
• Make a leadership chart to display on the wall. Add to the chart each time someone is a good leader. For example, "Megan is a good leader because she was the first to sit down and be quiet. She was giving a good example. Avik is a good leader because he praised his friend."